# Near or Far

by Wiley Blevins

a Capstone company—publishers for children
www.raintree.co.uk

Raintree is an imprint of Capstone Global Library Limited, a company incorporated in England and Wales having its registered office at 264 Banbury Road, Oxford, OX2 7DY – Registered company number: 6695582

www.raintree.co.uk
myorders@raintree.co.uk

Text © Capstone Global Library Limited 2020
The moral rights of the proprietor have been asserted.

All rights reserved. No part of this publication may be reproduced in any form or by any means (including photocopying or storing it in any medium by electronic means and whether or not transiently or incidentally to some other use of this publication) without the written permission of the copyright owner, except in accordance with the provisions of the Copyright, Designs and Patents Act 1988 or under the terms of a licence issued by the Copyright Licensing Agency, Saffron House, 6–10 Kirby Street, London EC1N 8TS (www.cla.co.uk). Applications for the copyright owner's written permission should be addressed to the publisher.

Edited by Erika Shores
Designed by Elyse White
Picture research by Tracy Cummins
Production by Laura Manthe
Originated by Capstone Global Library Limited
Printed and bound in India

ISBN 978 1 4747 6871 9 (hardback)
ISBN 978 1 4747 6886 3 (paperback)

**British Library Cataloguing in Publication Data**
A full catalogue record for this book is available from the British Library.

**Acknowledgements**
Shutterstock: Alexey Seafarer, 19, Bildagentur Zoonar GmbH, Cover Background, Doubletree Studio, 9, ESB Professional, 5, Ivan_Sabo, 7, Johan Swanepoel, Cover Left, kimson, 15, M. Cornelius, 13, MommaAbbott, Design Element, photolinc, Design Element, prattaph, 11, Tricia Daniel, 21, ZM_Photo, 17.

Every effort has been made to contact copyright holders of material reproduced in this book. Any omissions will be rectified in subsequent printings if notice is given to the publisher.

All the internet addresses (URLs) given in this book were valid at the time of going to press. However, due to the dynamic nature of the internet, some addresses may have changed, or sites may have changed or ceased to exist since publication. While the author and publisher regret any inconvenience this may cause readers, no responsibility for any such changes can be accepted by either the author or the publisher.

# Contents

Where is it?............4
In the desert............6
In forests and lakes......10
On other places.........18
    Glossary................22
    Find out more..........23
    Answers to questions......23
    Comprehension questions....24
    Index................24

# Where is it?

Look around.

What do you see?

The boat is near the beach.

The island is far away.

# In the desert

The chameleon is in the desert. It has found something to eat. It shoots out its long tongue. Yum! Yum!

The road goes through

the desert.

The tree is near the road.

The hills are far away.

# In forests and lakes

The deer is near the lake.

It is eating the grass.

Is the deer nearer to the lake or the trees?

The eagle flies near the forest. It is far from the ground. It flies high in the sky.

The boats are near the houses. They are in a harbour.

How many boats are there?

The mountains are far away.

The castle is far away.

It is on an island.

The castle is near the lake.

# On other places

The polar bears are on the ice. The mother bear is near the cub. The cub is near its mother. They stay close to each other.

The mountain is big and tall. It is far away. The flowers are near. They are pretty. What colour are the flowers?

# Glossary

**cub**  a young bear

**desert**  a place where not much rain falls

**harbour**  the part of a lake or sea near land where boats are kept safe

**island**  land that is completely surrounded by water

# Find out more

*Eddie and Ellie's Opposites at the Farm*, Rebecca Rissman (Raintree, 2013)

*Opposites!* (Look & Learn), National Geographic Kids (National Geographic Kids, 2012)

*Opposites* (Board Book), Penny West (Raintree, 2014)

# Website

www.bbc.com/bitesize/clips/zy26sbk
This BBC Bitesize video introduces the use of words to describe their location.

# Answers to questions

Here are the answers to the questions in the book: Page 10: the deer is nearer to the lake; Page 14: there are four boats; Page 20: the flowers are red.

# Comprehension questions

1. How is a desert different from a forest?

2. Why does the mother polar bear stay near her cub?

# Index

beach 4
boats 4, 14
castle 16
chameleon 6
deer 10
desert 6, 8
eagle 12
flowers 20
grass 10
harbour 14
hills 8
houses 14
ice 18
island 4
lake 10
mountains 16, 20
polar bears 18
road 8
sky 12
tree 8